CREATIVE COOKING

Quick & Easy Recipes

To: Darlene

JAY KINNEY

ACKNOWLEDGEMENTS

"Be so busy giving credit to others that you really don't need it for yourself."

I would like to thank a bunch of people for their efforts on this book. There's nothing more effective and rewarding than showing a genuine interest in other people. Katie Quinn has been a big help over on YouTube promoting my books. Check out her awesome channel, qkatie, for even more recipes.

A big shout out to Aaron Clarey, the man who gave me a swift kick in the ass about writing this book. The most important thing in life is other people. I can definitely relate to his simple message. I would have to say he is one of the best authors of our time.

I sincerely thank the following people for their images, Pawel Kadysz, Paulina Lohunko, Michal Kulesza, Terry Artt, Victoria Herrara, Michael Richert and Anthony Smolenski.

Last but not least, a big thanks to my Dad. After showing me how to draw food at the age of five, I was hooked. We would make subs, nachos, you name it. I will always remember the memories of spending time with him in the kitchen. The effects of having a really awesome father in life are infinite.

INTRODUCTION

"The greatest challenge in life is the wise use of all of our resources and to maximize our full potential."

I had to master this principle in order to become a chef. If you want to do something worthwhile in life, you have to push forward. It's all about making measurable progress in reasonable time. When you develop a better plan in your life (or even a recipe), you can really pour it on. Life responds to deserve not need.

I was very fortunate when I picked up a very valuable skill: cooking. It's something I would do for free. Cooking has led me to some wild places: the U.S. Army, Germany, Cuisine Magazine and even the Food Network.

Cooking food pays huge dividends for your health, easier said than done. To achieve great health, you have to pay the price. There are only two factors to consider with cooking on a regular basis. There is the pain of discipline or the pain of regret.

You could cook that meal, save some money and your waistline. Or you can pull up in the drive thru. I've never been a fan of fast food.

The really sad part about human nature is that we only do the minimum amount of work. You could do this, you could do that, but will you?

I can already hear it. I know buying produce and meat costs money. It takes time but hey it's your life. Read the books, walk around the block, go to the farmer's markets every Saturday. You really have no excuse here. As cheesy as it sounds, you are what you eat.

I may not be a doctor, but at least take a look at what you are eating. Today we are constantly bombarded with what's good and bad to eat. Ironically, stress and oxygen are two of the biggest threats to your health.

We are drowning in so much information and starving for wisdom. All I can say is that you need to examine your diet and think of it more like a lifestyle. Eat more fruits and vegetables, how hard is that? Skip meat a few days a week.

In order to live a good life, you need to eat very well. Use this book as a roadmap to all of your culinary adventures. Open up your mind and discover a whole new level of Creative Cooking!

TABLE OF CONTENTS

Vanilla Sauce

Wild Berry Sauce

Wild Berry Vinaigrette

BIG, THICK & JUICY SANDWICHES

Asian BBQ Pork

BBQ Chicken Wrap

Big Beefy Boss Burritos

Breakfast Burritos with Taco Bacon

Carnita Grilled Cheese

Cheeseburger Wrap

Chipotle Lime Chicken Quesadillas

French Chicken Salad

Grilled Portobello

Italian Beef Panini

Meyer Lemon Thyme Chicken Sandwich with Provolone

Mozzarella Meatball Subs

Nacho Beef Quesadillas

Parmesan Garlic Four-Cheese Panini

Shrimp Po'boy with Remoulade

Smoked Brisket Gyro

Smoked Salmon Sliders

Southwest Chicken Hani

Super Sloppy J's

BACON MAN

Bacon Boss Burritos

Bacon Boursin Mashed Potatoes

Bacon Boursin Risotto

Bacon Business Breakfast Sandwich

Bacon, Chicken & Ranch Quesadilla

Bacon Chicken Sliders

Bacon Fried Rice

Bacon Nachos

Bacon Quinoa Salad

Bacon Scramble

Candied Bacon

EASY ENTREES

Beef and Barley Stew

Beef Barbacoa

Beef Pasties

Bison Chili

Bison Quinoa Stuffed Peppers

Bulgogi

Chicken Cacciatore

Chipotle Lime Chicken

Crockpot Carnitas

Endless Empanadas

Garlic Herb Chicken Legs

Italian Pot Roast

Mango Braised Ribs

Ragin' Cajun Mac & Cheese

Roasted Cherry BBQ Chicken

Smoked Turkey & Wild Rice Soup

Southwest Chicken

Sunday Pot Roast

Tropical Chicken Stir Fry

SIDEKICKS

Aromatic Rice

Bison Gyoza

Broccoli Boursin Risotto Fritters

Garlic Cheese Biscuits

Garlic Herb Yukon Wedges

Kale with Garlic & Ginger

Pineapple Mango Chutney

Quick Quinoa

Saffron Rice

BONUS RECIPES

Andouille Sausage

Chorizo Sausage

Cinnamon Rolls

Granola

Honey Wheat Bread

Hot Cocoa Mix

Hummus

Indian Spice Mix

Italian Sausage

Rosemary Kalamata Olive Bread

Mango Coconut Oatmeal

Pumpkin Pie Scones

That Red Stuff

Turkey Pepperoni & Cheese Rolls

Ultimate Oatmeal

Wild Blueberry Muffins

CREATIVE COOKING

SUPERB SAUCES

Balsamic Vinaigrette

Makes 1 ⅓ cups

1 T. chopped garlic

1 T. chopped shallots

1 T. chopped basil

1 T. Dijon mustard

1 T. honey

1/3 c. balsamic vinegar

1 c. extra virgin olive oil

Kosher salt

Black pepper

Pulse the first eight ingredients in a blender. Slowly pour in the oil to emulsify. Chill for at least two hours before serving.

BBQ SAUCE

Makes 6 cups

¼ c. Worcestershire sauce

2 garlic cloves, smashed

½ c. unsulfured molasses

½ t. smoked paprika

2/3 c. light brown sugar

2 t. dry mustard powder

¼ c. apple cider vinegar

1/3 c. + 1 T. water

½ t. onion powder

½ t. ground cumin

24 oz. homemade ketchup

Bring all 11 ingredients to a boil. Simmer on low for 15 min.

CHERRY BBQ SAUCE

Makes 4 cups

3 c. homemade Ketchup

3/4 c cherry preserves*, Bonne Marie is my favorite

2 T. unsulfured molasses

2 T. light brown sugar

1 T. dry mustard powder

1 t. distilled white vinegar

1/2 t. smoked paprika

2 sprigs fresh thyme

Mix everything in a medium saucepan. Turn heat to low and cook for twenty minutes. Discard the thyme and puree in a food processor. This sauce works well with chicken, ribs and pork dishes.

*Cherries are really useful for promoting better sleep. They are full of phytochemicals, such as melatonin. Polyphenols come in cherries too. After a tough workout, consume cherries to boost exercise recovery.

CHIPOTLE SAUCE

Makes over 1 cup

1 c. Mexican crema or regular sour cream

3 T. buttermilk

1-3 T. adobo sauce from canned chipotle chilies

2 T. chopped cilantro

½ t. garlic powder

¼ t. kosher salt

Mix all six ingredients in a small bowl. Taste and adjust the spice level to suit your preference. Chill for up to 1 week.

CHIVE SAUCE

Makes 1 cup

8 oz. pkg. sour cream

3 T. water

3 T. minced chives

1 t. grated lemon zest, finely chopped

¼ t. kosher salt

½ t. black pepper

Mix and chill for at least 2 hours to mellow out the flavors. Serve with Smoked Salmon Sliders.

CONEY SAUCE

Makes 12 servings

2 lbs. ground sirloin

1 T. bacon fat

½ c. red bell peppers, finely chopped

1 large yellow onion, finely chopped

1 c. water

¼ c. Worcestershire sauce

2 (15 oz.) cans tomato sauce

2 t. dry mustard powder

2 t. chili powder

½ t. black pepper

1 t. smoked paprika

¼ c. light brown sugar

-

Brown off the beef in a medium saucepan on medium high heat. Drain the browned beef in a colander and set aside.

Sweat the onions and peppers in bacon fat for four minutes until the onions are translucent. Add the remaining ingredients and bring to a boil.

Reduce heat to medium low and cook uncovered for one hour. Taste and adjust the seasoning to your taste.

I prefer ground sirloin in this recipe because it is much leaner than ground chuck. Feel free to sub in venison or even bison for a wild take on a classic Coney sauce.

For a spicier Coney sauce, add chipotles in adobo. Remember always use chilies in moderation and wear gloves.

EASY TERIYAKI SAUCE

Makes 2 cups

1 c. tamari soy sauce

1 c. brown sugar

2 T. red wine vinegar

1 T. canola oil

2 t. minced garlic

2 t. minced ginger

Mix well and chill for a few hours. Drain off the garlic. Chill for up to 1 week or freeze for up to 3 months.

GREEN CHILE TEQUILA SAUCE

Makes 2 cups

1 (15 oz.) can green chilies

1 T. mayonnaise (I use Hellman's)

1 T. minced garlic

1 t. cayenne pepper

1 t. That Red Stuff (See BONUS RECIPES)

2 T. chopped scallions

1/3 c. honey

½ c. tequila

(Guys keep your clothes on, save the bottle of tequila for the ladies! If it is Tequila Tuesday, ask yourself if you have hugged your toilet today!)

Kosher salt

Black pepper

Blend everything together until it's smooth. Chill for at least two hours to mellow out the flavors. Serve with shrimp cocktail.

HONEY MUSTARD

Makes 3/4 cup

½ c. spicy brown mustard

½ c. orange blossom honey

Dash of cinnamon

Dash of turmeric

Dash of black pepper

Mix everything in a small bowl. Chill overnight to mellow out the flavors. Serve with chicken, fries or sandwiches.

HORSERADISH COLESLAW DRESSING

Makes 2 cups

1 ½ c. mayonnaise

¾ c. apple cider vinegar

2 T. Dijon mustard

2 T. honey

2 T. prepared horseradish

1 T. Sriracha (Chinese chili garlic sauce)

1 T. celery seed

1 t. That Red Stuff

¼ t. onion powder

Kosher salt

Black pepper

Whisk the dressing together in a mixing bowl.

For horseradish coleslaw, mix:

1 head green cabbage, thinly sliced

½ head red cabbage, thinly sliced

1 red bell pepper, thinly sliced

1 large carrot, grated

1 bunch scallions, thinly sliced

Mix the slaw and dressing together. Chill for at least 2 hours to let the flavors mellow out.

-

HORSERADISH CREAM SAUCE

Makes 1 cup

1 c. sour cream

1 T. heavy cream

1 T. sliced chives

2 T. prepared horseradish

Kosher salt

Black Pepper

Whisk everything in a small bowl. Chill for at least 2 hours to mellow out the flavors. Serve with beef!

This was a simple recipe that I learned in culinary school. Often, I was running a busy carving station with this sauce. Slather this sauce on beef and wedge between slider buns, hmmm!

KETCHUP

Makes 6 cups

2 T. extra virgin olive oil

½ large Spanish onion, finely chopped

2 garlic cloves, finely chopped

1 T. + ½ t. Hungarian paprika

1 T. chili powder

2 t. kosher salt

1 ¼ t. ground cinnamon

½ t. ground cloves

½ t. ground cumin

½ t. dry mustard powder

¼ t. black pepper

3 (28 oz.) cans whole tomatoes, drained, crushed

⅓ c. honey

⅓ c. light brown sugar

¼ c. apple cider vinegar

¼ c. white distilled vinegar

Heat the oil in a large saucepot on medium heat. Sweat the onions for five minutes. Add the garlic and cook two minutes. Add the spices and cook for one minute to wake up the aromatic elements. Add the tomatoes.

Cover and simmer on low for 25 min. Puree in a food processor or with an immersion blender. Put the sauce back on low heat. Stir in the honey, vinegars and brown sugar. Stir and cook on low heat uncovered for 30 min. Be extremely careful with this sauce. Do not turn up the heat at this stage; it will splatter all over your stove so keep an eye on it.

Cool completely and use within two weeks. Or use to make Cherry BBQ Sauce. It's time to upgrade your cooking skills. Commercially made ketchup is pumped full of high fructose corn syrup.

Studies have shown its damaging effects on the brain. Who wants chunks of brain lying on the floor? It has negative consequences very similar to excessive alcohol.

Do your body and your roasted potato wedges a favor, make some homemade ketchup.

MANGO SAUCE

Makes 2 cups

2 T. canola oil

2 c. frozen mango chunks

1 T. ground cumin

½ T. ground cinnamon

1 T. honey

½ T. Thai Chile sauce

1 T. cider vinegar

1 T. pickled ginger

Water

Heat the oil in a large skillet on medium heat. Add the mango and heat briefly just to thaw it out. Process everything in a blender until its smooth. Chill for at least two hours. Serve with eggrolls or pot stickers.

MARINARA SAUCE

Makes 1 quart

2 T. extra virgin olive oil

½ c finely chopped yellow onions

1 T. finely chopped garlic

1 bay leaf

2 (28 oz.) cans whole tomatoes with juice, crushed

¼ c. tomato paste

2 T. granulated sugar

2 t. dried oregano

2 t. dried thyme

Kosher salt

Black pepper

Heat a medium saucepan on medium heat. Cook the onions and garlic in oil for three minutes. Add the remaining ingredients. Bring to a simmer, reduce to medium low and simmer uncovered for twenty- five minutes. Discard the bay leaf. Taste and adjust the seasoning.

For Meat Sauce, brown off 1 lb. Italian sausage. Drain and add to the sauce after cooking the onions and garlic. You may also use ground beef, bison or venison.

MR. SMOKEY'S SALSA

Makes 4 cups

1 (28 oz.) can whole Italian tomatoes

1 (14.5 oz.) can fire roasted tomatoes

1-2 chipotles in adobo sauce, finely chopped

1 yellow onion, finely chopped

½ bunch cilantro, finely chopped

½ t. ground cumin

1 garlic clove, minced

Juice of 1 lime

Kosher Salt

Soak the diced onions in lime juice for 2 hrs. Drain and mix all ingredients in a bowl.

PARMESAN GARLIC SAUCE

Makes 1 ¼ cups

1 c. mayonnaise

3 T. grated Parmesan cheese

3 T. water

2 T. minced garlic

1 T. buttermilk

1 t. distilled white vinegar

1 t. dried thyme, crushed

1 t. dried oregano, crushed

1 t. dried basil, crushed

Kosher salt

Black pepper

Mix everything in a small bowl. Chill for at least two hours. Serve with sandwiches, fries or chicken wings. Use within three days.

-

RANCH DRESSING

Makes 1 ½ cups

1 c. mayonnaise

⅓ c. + 1 T. buttermilk

2 T. finely sliced scallions

1 T. minced parsley

1 t. minced garlic

½ t. white distilled vinegar

¼ t. kosher salt

Black pepper

Mix and chill for at least 2 hours. Serve with salads, pizza, chicken, etc. Use within three days.

RASPBERRY COCKTAIL SAUCE

Makes 2 cups

⅔ c. chili sauce

⅔ c. ketchup

¼ c. seedless raspberry preserves

2 T. prepared horseradish

1 T. Worcestershire sauce

¼ t. Tabasco sauce

Juice of 1 Meyer lemon

Kosher salt

Black pepper

Mix everything in a small bowl. Chill for at least two hours to mellow out the flavors. Serve with shrimp.

-

REMOULADE

Makes 2 ¼ cups

2 c. mayonnaise

2 T. ketchup

2 T. spicy brown mustard

1 T. chopped parsley

1 T. cayenne pepper

1 T. Meyer lemon juice

2 t. prepared horseradish

2 t. minced fresh garlic

1 t. Worcestershire sauce

1 t. celery salt

1 t. Hungarian paprika

1 chipotle in adobo, chopped

Process everything in a blender or food processor until its smooth, thin down with water if necessary. Chill for at least two hours to mellow out the flavors. Serve with crab cakes or shrimp.

RUM CARAMEL

Makes 2 ½ cups

½ lb. unsalted butter

1 ½ c. heavy cream

2 c. brown sugar

1 vanilla bean, split

1 cinnamon stick, crushed

¼ c. dark rum or bourbon whisky

Melt the butter on low heat in a medium saucepan. Off heat, whisk in the sugar and cream. Reduce down on medium heat to the desired consistency. Add the rum and leave for five minutes.

This sauce should coat the back of a spoon. Strain out the vanilla bean and cinnamon stick. Use this sauce within one week.

SPICY SOY SAUCE

Makes 2 ½ cups

2 c. water

2 c. low sodium soy sauce

½ c. rice wine vinegar, unseasoned

(Seasoned rice vinegar is way too salty)

½ c. pickled ginger juice

2 T. cayenne pepper

1 T. cornstarch + 1 T. water

Reduce the first five items down slightly in a medium saucepan. Once it comes to a boil, whisk in the cornstarch slurry. Bring back to a boil and reduce down to the desired consistency. Serve with eggrolls or pot stickers.

TANGY TANGERINE SAUCE

Makes 1 ¼ cups

¾ c. fresh tangerine juice

½ c. tamari

⅓ c. orange blossom honey

1 T. chopped scallions

2 t. grated tangerine zest

1 t. chopped garlic

1 t. chopped ginger

1 Saigon cinnamon stick, crushed

Mix everything in a medium saucepan. Bring to a boil. Reduce heat and cook for 8-10 minutes. Strain and chill for at least two hours. Serve with eggrolls, chicken or steak.

THAI CHILE & GINGER VINAIGRETTE

Makes 2 ¾ cups

2 T. pickled ginger

2 c. canola oil

½ c. rice wine vinegar

¼ c. Thai Chile sauce

2 t. minced lemongrass

2 t. toasted sesame oil

2 T. minced chives

Process everything in a blender or food processor until it's emulsified. Adjust the acidity or amount of sesame oil to taste. Chill for at least two hours. Serve with coleslaw or salads.

VANILLA SAUCE

Makes 3 cups

12 large eggs, separated

1 qt. heavy whipping cream

2 vanilla beans, split and scraped

1 3/4 c. granulated sugar

Bring an inch of water to a boil in a medium saucepan. Whisk the eggs, cream, vanilla and sugar in a large metal mixing bowl. Put the bowl on top and drop to a simmer on medium heat. Whisk every few minutes until it reaches 168 degrees. This sauce should coat the back of a spoon.

Strain and discard the vanilla beans. Chill for at least two hours. Serve with bread pudding or soufflés.

-

WILD BERRY SAUCE

Makes 1 ½ cups

2 c. frozen wild berries, thawed

½ c. granulated sugar

3 T. raspberry schnapps

2 sprigs fresh thyme

Pinch of red chili flakes

Mix the berries, sugar and schnapps. Chill for at least two hours.
Pour into a large skillet and bring to a boil. Add the thyme sprigs.
Boil for 2 minutes so that it can coat the back of a spoon. Strain
and add the chili flakes.

This sauce is fantastic with salmon.

WILD BERRY VINAIGRETTE

Makes 2 cups

1 c. frozen wild berries, thawed

½ c. honey

½ c. water

¼ c. balsamic vinegar

2 T. chopped shallots

1 T. chopped fresh garlic

Kosher salt

Black pepper

Extra virgin olive oil

Process the first eight ingredients until it's smooth. Slowly pour in the olive oil to emulsify the vinaigrette.

Generally, vinaigrettes use a one-part vinegar to three parts oil ratio. I use significantly less oil to taste. However, do not overdo it on the oil, less is more.

JAY KINNEY

-

BIG, THICK & JUICY SANDWICHES

ASIAN BBQ PORK

Makes 6 c. sauce and 11 c. pulled pork

¼ c. Worcestershire sauce

2 garlic cloves, smashed

½ c. unsulfured molasses

½ t. smoked paprika

2/3 c. light brown sugar

2 t. dry mustard powder

¼ c. apple cider vinegar

1/3 c. + 1 T. water

½ t. onion powder

½ t. ground cumin

24 oz. homemade ketchup

7-7 ½ lb. pork butt

1 c. That Red Stuff, divided

-

3 oz. Hawaiian ginger, peeled, sliced

2 stalks lemongrass, smashed

Zest of ½ orange

Bring the first 11 ingredients to a boil. Simmer on low for 15 min. Toss the garlic and puree. Cool completely. Cut ½" slits all along the pork and insert the ginger. Pop the pork in a large bowl. Pour 1/3 cup of the seasoning mix onto the pork. With gloves, massage the rub in. (If not your hands will turn red!) Cover and chill for at least 2 hours.

Spray the inside of a large crockpot with nonstick spray. Add the pork, lemongrass and orange zest. Mix 3 cups BBQ sauce with 2 cups water. Pour the sauce mixture over the pork. Cover and cook on low heat for 8 hours. Drain off the juice and wipe the crockpot clean. Spray with nonstick spray. Shred the pork and add back to the pot. Add 1/3 cup seasoning and BBQ sauce to taste.

Cover and cook on low for 2 hours. Serve with pretzel buns and slaw.

BBQ CHICKEN WRAP

Makes 1 serving

8" flour tortilla

2 T. smoked cheddar cheese, shredded

1 T. each: pepperoncini's, red onions and cooked bacon, finely chopped

2 T. rotisserie chicken, cooled, finely chopped

Cherry BBQ Sauce

Heat a griddle pan on medium heat. Heat a small skillet on medium high heat. Add 2 t. olive oil to each pan. Sauté the pepperoncini's, onions and bacon for 2-3 min. until the onions are translucent.

Meanwhile add the cheese to the tortilla in the griddle pan. Add the chicken to the sautéed mix. Pour over the tortilla and add the BBQ sauce. Roll up like a burrito, cut and serve.

Variation: You can experiment with different sauces to ramp up the flavor. Try ranch, parmesan garlic sauce or honey mustard in place of the BBQ sauce. Be a boss and pick a sauce!

-

BIG BEEFY BOSS BURRITOS

Makes 1 serving

8" flour tortilla

2 T. Mexican cheese, shredded

6 oz. ground chuck or sirloin

2 T. red onion, finely chopped

2 T. red bell pepper, finely chopped

2 T. jalapenos, finely chopped

2 T. cooked bacon, chopped

½ t. chili powder

½ t. smoked paprika

2 T. Ranch dressing + 2 t. adobo sauce from canned chipotles

Heat a griddle pan and a medium skillet on medium heat. Brown off the beef in the skillet until it is browned off and cooked through. Add the onions and peppers. Cook 2 min. Meanwhile add the cheese to the tortilla in the griddle pan.

Add the bacon to the beef and heat through for 1 min. Season with chili powder and smoked paprika. Pour over the tortilla and add the Chipotle Ranch. Roll up and eat.

Note: I like my food spicy but you can omit the jalapenos if they make you cry.

JAY KINNEY

BREAKFAST BURRITOS WITH

TACO BACON

Makes 1 serving

8" tortilla

Mexican cheese, shredded

Thick cut bacon, cooked, cooled and chopped

Low sodium taco seasoning

Scrambled eggs, cooled slightly

Roasted red peppers, diced and patted dry

Scallions, thinly sliced

Heat your oven to 350. Line a baking sheet with parchment paper. Lay out a few strips of bacon (I lay out the whole pack and eat it throughout the day). Season liberally with taco seasoning.

Cook until its crispy, drain off and save the grease (in case you want to drink it). Chop up the bacon and set aside. Heat a griddle pan on medium heat. Add 2 t. bacon fat and add the tortilla. Sprinkle some cheese on top. Quickly microwave the eggs briefly, just to heat them up. Add the peppers, scallions and bacon. Mix and pour over the tortilla. Roll up and enjoy. Serve with salsa and sour cream.

48

CARNITA GRILLED CHEESE

Makes 11 cups pork

7-8 lb. pork butt, trimmed

½ c. That Red Stuff

8 garlic cloves

2 bay leaves

1 (28 oz.) can Enchilada sauce

2 Persian limes, juiced

2 T. light brown sugar

1 yellow onion, sliced

1 chipotle in adobo + 2 T. sauce

Chicken stock

Sliced challah bread

Smoked Gouda cheese, shredded

Rub the pork with taco seasoning. Cut 8 small slits all over the pork. Stuff with fresh garlic. Cover and cook on low for 8-9 hrs. Chop and cool.

Heat a griddle pan on medium heat. Butter two slices of challah bread. Lay them in the pan with the cheese. Add the carnitas and cover with a large lid. After 2 minutes the cheese should be melted. Cut and serve.

CHEESEBURGER WRAP

Makes 1 serving

6-7 oz. ground sirloin

1 T. bacon fat

8" flour tortilla

2 T. smoked cheddar cheese, shredded

2 T. onions, finely chopped

1 T. tomatoes, finely chopped

1 T. finely chopped pickles

Ketchup

Mustard

Heat a medium skillet on medium high heat. Add the bacon fat, onions and the ground sirloin. Brown off until there is no pink. Season and keep warm.

Heat a griddle pan on medium heat. Add a small amount of olive oil along with the tortilla. Add your cheese and sit there patiently until it melts. Transfer the tortilla to a cutting board. Add your beef mixture, tomatoes, pickles, ketchup and mustard in that order.

CHIPOTLE LIME CHICKEN

QUESADILLAS

Makes 6-8 servings

1 c. fresh lime juice

2 T. chipotles in adobo sauce

½ t. smoked paprika

1 T. honey

1 t. roasted garlic powder

½ t. cumin

2 T. olive oil

½ t. kosher salt

6 boneless skinless chicken breasts

Puree the first 8 items in a blender. Pour into a bowl and add the chicken. Chill and marinate overnight. Leave the chicken out at room temperature for 30 min.

Heat oven to 375 and line a baking sheet with parchment paper. Drain off and discard the marinade. Roast the chicken off until it is 165. Rest for 10 min. then slice.

51

-

Note: You may butterfly the chicken to cook it faster. Without cutting your hand off, use a sharp boning knife and cut the chicken horizontally. Use the tip of the knife to open up the chicken like a book. You are the chicken surgeon! This is a totally optional step but bonus points for being a boss.

For each quesadilla:

⅓ c. Chipotle Lime chicken, cooked, cooled and chopped

2 T. roasted red peppers, finely chopped, patted dry

2 T. finely chopped onions, sautéed

8" flour tortilla

3 T. Mexican cheese, shredded

Heat a griddle pan on medium high heat. Spray with nonstick spray. Add the tortilla and top with cheese. Nuke the chicken, peppers and onions in a bowl for 30 seconds. Pour over the tortilla and fold over. Use a big sandwich press and lay on top. Flip and press the other side briefly, do not burn. Cut and serve at once.

FRENCH CHICKEN SALAD

Makes 6 servings

1 c. Hellman's mayo

¼ c. Dijon mustard

½ c. celery, small dice

½ t. roasted garlic powder

3 T. scallions, thinly sliced (only the green tops)

Kosher salt

Black pepper

4 c. rotisserie chicken, cooked, cooled and chopped

Mix the mayo, mustard, celery, garlic, scallions, salt and pepper. Adjust the seasoning to your taste. Fold in the chicken. Chill for at least 4 hours.

Serve with croissants.

-

GRILLED PORTOBELLO

Makes 4 servings

¼ c. olive oil

¼ c. + 2 T. balsamic reduction

¼ c. + 2 T. tamari soy sauce

2 T. roasted garlic powder

2 T. dried thyme, crushed

½ c. water

Kosher salt

Black pepper

4 Portobello mushrooms, stems removed

Blend the first 8 items. (This marinade can also be used for chicken, steak or pork.) Add the portabellas, marinate for 1 hr. Grill until the mushroom is cooked through to taste. Cool and pour marinade over top.

Serve on grilled ciabatta bread with Gouda cheese. Use within 3 days.

ITALIAN BEEF PANINI

Makes 6-8 servings

4 1/2 lbs. beef chuck roast

Kosher salt

Black pepper

1 onion, chopped

4 carrots, chopped

4 celery ribs, chopped

8 garlic cloves, crushed

1 bunch fresh thyme

28 oz. can whole tomatoes, crushed

¼ t each: ground allspice, cinnamon and cloves

2 bay leaves

1 ½ c. Shiraz red wine

½ c beef stock

-

Season the beef with salt and pepper. Sear off in a cast iron Dutch oven with olive oil on med high heat. Once they are browned, lay them into your large crockpot.

Sauté the onions for 6 min. Add the carrots, celery, garlic and thyme. Sauté for 2 min. Add spices and bay leaves. Raise heat to high and deglaze with the wine.

Cook down for 5 min. Add the stock and tomatoes, bring to a boil. Pour over the beef and cook on low for 8-9 hours. Chop into pieces and set aside.

Heat a griddle pan on medium high heat. Spray with nonstick spray. Open up a half moon ciabatta bread. Add the mozzarella, tomatoes from the crockpot and the beef. Lay the ciabatta in the pan and smash with a sandwich press. Brown on both sides to melt the cheese.

MEYER LEMON THYME CHICKEN SANDWICH WITH PROVOLONE

Makes 10-12 sandwiches

1 t. kosher salt

½ t. black pepper

4 thyme sprigs, chopped

1 T. garlic, minced

Juice of 5 Meyer lemons

3 T. extra virgin olive oil

2 T. honey

6 boneless skinless chicken breasts

Mix up the marinade and add a few of the used lemon halves. Add the chicken and mix. Cover and chill overnight. Heat oven to 350. Line a baking sheet with parchment paper.

Heat a large sauté pan on medium high heat. Add 2 T. olive oil. Pat the chicken dry and discard the marinade. Brown off the chicken on both sides in 2 batches.

-

Lay the chicken out on the prepared baking sheet. Bake the chicken briefly until they reach 165. Rest for 15 min. before slicing against the grain. I like to build sandwiches with brioche buns and provolone cheese. Really the sky is the limit with chicken, add whatever suits you.

*This chicken is wonderful in a cold wrap too. Slice the chicken and top with Thai Chile slaw in a spinach wrap. I made it at work and six wraps vanished. Very tasty!

Note: Remember to always wear disposable gloves when handling raw chicken and pretty much any other raw meat. To prevent cross contamination, use Clorox wipes to wipe down all surfaces. Don't forget to wash your hands.

You don't want the chicken police coming after you. We all have heard about the duck face police. They are trying to "quack" down on those duck faces on social media.

MOZZARELLA MEATBALL SUBS

Makes 5 or 6 sandwiches

2 t. extra virgin olive oil

2 t. bacon fat

1 medium onion, finely chopped

1 red bell pepper, finely chopped

1 ½ t. minced garlic

3 slices whole wheat bread, crumbled

½ c. + 2 T. grated Parmesan cheese

1 ½ t. each: dried basil, dried thyme and dried oregano

Kosher salt

Black Pepper

1 large egg + 1 large egg yolk

1 ½ lbs. ground pork

1 ½ lbs. ground sirloin

1 lb. fresh mozzarella, chopped into bite size pieces

Sub rolls

Marinara

JAY KINNEY

-

Heat a large skillet on medium heat. Sweat the onions and peppers in the olive oil and bacon fat for five minutes. Add the garlic and cook for two minutes. Pour into a large bowl and cool completely. Add the remaining ingredients, not the mozzarella. Cover and chill for at least two hours to mellow out the flavors.

Heat oven to 375. Line a large baking sheet with foil. Portion out the meatballs with a medium ice cream scoop. Make a small indentation in each one and stuff with the mozzarella. Bake for 25-30 minutes or until they are 160 degrees. Cool for 5 minutes. Serve on sub rolls with marinara and mozzarella.

Mama Mia!

NACHO BEEF QUESADILLAS

Makes 1 serving

1/3 c. cooked ground beef, drained

1 t. bacon fat

2 T. low sodium taco seasoning

1 t. smoked paprika

2 T. roasted red peppers, patted dry

2 T. sautéed onions

3 T. Mexican cheese, shredded

8" flour tortilla

Heat a griddle pan on medium heat. Grease with bacon fat and spread. Add the tortilla and cheese. Briefly nuke the beef, seasoning, paprika, peppers and onions for 30 sec. on high heat with Chef Mike. Pour over the tortilla and fold over. Lay a sandwich press on top to make a tight, firm quesadilla.

Cut and go. Serve with salsa and sour cream.

PARMESAN GARLIC FOUR-CHEESE PANINI

Makes 1 serving

2 thin slices Cheddar cheese

2 thin slices Fontina cheese

2 thin slices Gouda cheese

2 T. Parmesan Garlic Sauce

1 Half-moon ciabatta bread

Heat a griddle pan on medium heat. Grease with nonstick spray. Lay the ciabatta down and top with cheeses. Add the garlic sauce and weigh down with a sandwich press. Brown on both sides and serve at once.

Note: You can add or subtract the cheeses. Mix it up and experiment with your food.

SHRIMP PO'BOY WITH REMOULADE

Makes 1 serving

Frozen popcorn shrimp

Sliced dill pickles, patted dry

Shredded lettuce

Sliced tomatoes, preferably heirloom striped tomatoes*

Remoulade Sauce

1 (8") sub roll

Fill a 5 qt. cast iron Dutch oven halfway with peanut or canola oil. (Remember heat will expand the oil once you add food so do not overfill the pot.) Deep fry the popcorn shrimp until they are golden brown and cooked through.

Meanwhile heat a griddle pan to medium. Cut the sub roll in half horizontally and butter. Weigh down with a sandwich press to get a golden brown crust. Spread the remoulade sauce on the roll. Add the shrimp, lettuce, tomato and pickles. Sauce the top and you are all set.

*Heirloom tomatoes can usually be found at your local farmer's market. Don't worry they will taste great. If you are a next level boss, you can grow your own tomatoes. Fantastic and cheap!

SMOKED BRISKET GYRO

Makes 1 serving

3 oz. smoked beef brisket, chopped

Shredded lettuce

Tomatoes, finely chopped

Finely chopped pepperoncini's

Feta cheese

Parmesan Garlic Sauce

Greek pita bread

Heat a small skillet on medium high heat. Add olive oil and the beef. Briefly heat through and set aside. Heat a griddle pan to medium heat. Grease with nonstick spray and add the pita. You want the bread to be warm and pliable but not crispy.

Lay out a square sheet of foil. Add your lettuce, tomato, beef, pepperoncini, feta and garlic sauce. Roll the gyro and secure the bottom. The foil will keep the sandwich hot. Serve at once.

Opa!

SMOKED SALMON SLIDERS

Makes 1 serving

Sour cream

Kosher salt

Black pepper

Lemon zest, grated

Minced chives

Smoked salmon

Arugula

Red bell pepper, julienned

Sub rolls

Mix up the first 5 ingredients. Use your imagination and taste your creation. You can use dill in place of chive, add hot sauce, etc. Briefly sauté the salmon just to heat it through. Split a roll and warm it in the microwave. Add the salmon, arugula, red pepper and chive sauce.

This is a fairly easy way to get your fish and veggies. Salmon is loaded with omega-3, vitamin B12, vitamin D and protein. Besides bacon, I would have to say that salmon is one of my favorite foods.

SOUTHWEST CHICKEN HANI

Makes 6-8 servings

1 T. chili powder

2 t. each: dried oregano, dried thyme, roasted garlic powder, onion powder, smoked paprika, kosher salt

1 t. black pepper

¼ c. olive oil

6 boneless skinless chicken breasts

Smoked cheddar cheese, shredded

Cooked bacon, chopped

Roasted red peppers, chopped, patted dry

Ranch Dressing or Chipotle Ranch

Mix up the marinade and add the chicken. Cover and chill overnight. Roast at 375 on a parchment lined baking sheet until the chicken is at 165. Rest for at least 10 min. before slicing.

Heat a griddle pan on medium heat. Grease with nonstick spray. Add the tortilla and shredded smoked cheddar. Briefly sauté the bacon, chicken and roasted peppers. Pour over the tortilla. Add your spicy sauce (ranch + chipotles). Roll and go.

SUPER SLOPPY J'S

Makes 6-8 servings

1 T. olive oil

2 lbs. ground bison

1 large sweet onion, finely chopped

1 red bell pepper, finely chopped

1 T. minced garlic

1 tsp. dried thyme

¼ c. light brown sugar

2 c. tomato sauce

1 T. Worcestershire sauce

2 T. prepared yellow mustard

2 T. tomato paste

Montreal Steak seasoning

Brown off the bison in a large skillet on medium heat. Drain and set aside. Put the large skillet back on medium heat. Sweat the onions and peppers in olive oil until the onions are translucent. Add the garlic and thyme, cook 2 min. Add the bison and remaining items. Cover and simmer for 30 minutes (Uncover and cook longer for a drier mix).

Serve on Kaiser or Brioche buns.

JAY KINNEY

BACON MAN

Are you bringing home the bacon?

Bacon is my favorite food, just above sweet potatoes. So far, I have converted six full blown vegans to the magical land of bacon. I guess my new bacon suit really sealed the deal. Who could resist a man in a bacon suit? No more tree hugging for them!

Who doesn't love bacon? I prefer a thick cut bacon, such as Wright's. This brand can be found in most big box supermarkets and it even comes in 3 lb. packages at Meijer's! There is thick cut, low sodium, you name it. However, I hear some of you now.

Turkey bacon is not real bacon, just play dough strips. Beef bacon is not real bacon, just a thousand rubber bands. Do the pig farmers a favor and buy real bacon. It is rich in choline, a vital nutrient for brain development. Time to add bacon to your brain food list.

Let's think of bacon as a Christmas present; it's the food that keeps on giving. Save that grease! I would highly recommend everyone to have about one gallon, minimum, of bacon grease in their fridge at all times. I mix olive oil with it when I sauté foods.

BACON BEEF HOAGIES

Makes 1 serving

2 T. bacon fat

8 oz. ground sirloin

Mrs. Dash's salt-free hamburger seasoning

8" sesame hoagie roll

1 slice smoked provolone

3 T. cooked bacon, chopped

Heat oven to 250. Heat a medium skillet to medium high heat. Add the bacon fat and the beef. Smash down with a spatula and add the hamburger seasoning. Wash your hands to prevent cross contamination. Any time you handle raw meat, you should wash your hands. Make sure you actually use warm water, not that ice cold water.

Meanwhile, split the hoagie roll but leave on the "hinge." Add the cheese and pop in the oven. To serve, cut the burger in half. Lay the beef on the roll and top with bacon. Everything is better with bacon.

-

BACON BOSS BURRITOS

Makes 1 serving

8" flour tortilla

2 T. Mexican cheese, shredded

6 oz. ground chuck or sirloin

2 T. red onion, finely chopped

2 T. red bell pepper, finely chopped

2 T. jalapenos, finely chopped

2 T. cooked bacon, chopped

½ t. chili powder

½ t. smoked paprika

2 T. Ranch dressing + 2 t. adobo sauce from canned chipotles

Heat a griddle pan and a medium skillet on medium heat. Brown off the beef in the skillet until it is browned off and cooked through. Add the onions and peppers. Cook 2 min. Meanwhile add the cheese to the tortilla in the griddle pan. Add the bacon to the beef and heat through for 1 min. Season with chili powder and smoked paprika. Pour over the tortilla and add the Chipotle Ranch. Roll up and eat.

BACON BOURSIN MASHED POTATOES

Makes 4-6 servings

3-4 lbs. Yukon potatoes, peeled, chopped

½ stick unsalted butter

1 (5.2 oz.) pkg. Boursin cheese

1 T. fresh thyme, chopped

1 bunch chives, minced

Kosher salt

Black pepper

½ c. whole milk

1 c. cooked bacon, chopped

Add the potatoes to a large stock pot. Add cold water and cover. Bring to a rapid boil. Usually the potatoes will take at least 20 min. Once they are fork tender, drain in a large colander. Shake off all of the excess water.

Pour the potatoes back into the pot and heat to a very low heat. Add the remaining items.

JAY KINNEY

BACON BOURSIN RISOTTO

Makes 4-6 servings

5-5 ½ c. low sodium chicken stock

2 T. bacon fat

1/3 c. shallots, minced

1 ½ c. Arborio rice (short grain Italian rice)

1 (5.2 oz.) pkg. Boursin cheese

1/3 c. mascarpone cheese

2 T. minced chives

½ c. cooked bacon, finely chopped

Heat stock just below a simmer on medium heat. In a medium saucepot, heat the bacon fat to medium high heat. Sauté the shallots until they are translucent, 2-3 min. Add the rice and toast for 2 min.

Stir in ½ c. stock. Continue to stir in ½ c. additions of stock. The rice should be al dente, but not crunchy, after 25 min. Off heat, stir in the cheeses, chives and bacon.

BACON BUSINESS BREAKFAST

SANDWICH

Makes 1 serving

3 frozen waffles, preferably pumpkin spice

3 T. Biscoff (Belgian cookie dough spread)

3 T. Smart Balance peanut butter

3 slices thick cut bacon, cooked

Toast the waffles on setting 3 (most toaster have 5 settings). Flip and toast on setting 0 (this helps to ensure a dry, crispy texture). Lay one waffle on a plate. Spread with Biscoff and peanut butter. Cut the bacon in half and lay on top. Repeat with the last two waffles. Have the milk ready and dive in!

Or if you wake up in a gutter, douse it in pure maple syrup for a massive sugar rush!

-

Bacon, Chicken & Ranch Quesadilla

Makes 1 serving

1 T. bacon fat

8" flour tortilla

3 T. Mexican cheese, shredded

⅓ c. rotisserie chicken, cooled and chopped

2 T. cooked bacon, finely chopped

2 T. finely chopped onions, sautéed

2 T. Ranch dressing

Heat a griddle pan on medium high heat. Smear bacon fat all over the pan. Add the tortilla and top with cheese. Nuke the chicken, bacon and onions in a bowl for 30 seconds.

Pour over the tortilla and sprinkle the dressing on top. Fold over and lay a big sandwich press on top. Flip and press the other side briefly, do not burn. Cut and serve at once with salsa and sour cream.

BACON CHICKEN SLIDERS

Makes 1 serving

2 T. bacon fat

2 Brioche rolls, split

3 T. Ranch Dressing

2 t. Adobo sauce*

1 T. chopped parsley

4 oz. rotisserie chicken, sliced

3 thick cut bacon slices, cooked, cut in half

2 slices smoked cheddar cheese

Heat a griddle pan to medium heat. Add 2 T. bacon fat and smear all over. Mix the ranch, adobo sauce and parsley; set aside. Lay the brioche buns on one side of the pan. Lay the chicken slices on the other side, overlapping them slightly. After 1 minute, flip and add the bacon and cheese.

Flip the rolls and top with the bacon-chicken mixture. Add the spicy ranch sauce and top bun. Time to slide right into the southwest!

*Adobo sauce is from canned chipotle chilies. Chipotles chilies are smoked red jalapenos.

BACON FRIED RICE

Makes 4 servings

6 slices thick cut bacon

2 T. bacon fat

¼ c. yellow onions, chopped

¼ c. red bell peppers, chopped

2 c. cooked brown or white rice

2 large eggs, beaten

1/3 c. frozen peas, thawed

Tamari (Japanese soy sauce)

Heat a large nonstick skillet or wok on medium heat. Cook the bacon until it's crispy. Chop and set aside. Raise the heat to medium high. Add the bacon fat, peppers and onions. Stir-fry until the onions are translucent.

Add the rice and stir-fry for 2 min. Make and well in the middle of the rice. Pour in the eggs and cook 2 min. Stir in the peas and bacon. Season with tamari sauce.

BACON NACHOS

Makes 4-6 servings

4 c. Mexican cheese, shredded

3 c. Asian BBQ pork, chopped

1 c. cooked bacon, chopped

1 bag tortilla chips

½ c. scallions, sliced

½ c. Heirloom tomatoes, chopped

4 jalapenos, chopped

Grease a large roasting pan with nonstick cooking spray. Layer the chips, pork, tomatoes, jalapenos, scallions, cheese and bacon in that order. Repeat. Bake at 350 for 10 min. You may leave out the jalapenos if you're scared.

BACON QUINOA SALAD

Makes 4-6 servings

2 c. white quinoa, cooked, cooled

½ c. thick cut bacon, cooked, chopped

½ c. red bell peppers, chopped

3 T. scallions, sliced

1 T. chili powder

2 t. smoked paprika

1 t. ground cumin

½ t. dried thyme

Mix everything in a mixing bowl. Chill for at least 4 hours to mellow out the flavors. Serve with any entrée.

BACON SCRAMBLE

Makes 2 servings

5 thick cut bacon slices

2 Yukon gold potatoes, baked, chopped

2/3 c. chopped shallots

2/3 c. chopped red peppers

Smoked paprika

Dried oregano

Chili powder

Garlic powder

Ground cumin

4 eggs

3 T. Mexican cheese, shredded

-

Chop up the bacon into small pieces. Add to a 10" cast iron skillet. Cook on medium heat until the fat has rendered out and the bacon is crisp. Save 2 T. fat and set the cooked bacon off to a small bowl.

Raise your heat to medium high. Heat up a large nonstick skillet. Add the shallots and peppers. Cook for 4-5 min. until the shallots are translucent but not brown. Add the potatoes and seasonings. Cook for 2 min. Make a well and add 1 T. bacon fat. Pour in the eggs and scramble to taste. Add the cheese and serve at once.

CANDIED BACON

Makes 4-6 servings

½ c. granulated sugar

¼ c. unsulphured molasses

2 t. ground cinnamon

12 oz. low sodium bacon, preferably Kirkland Signature

Heat oven to 350. Mix the sugar, molasses and cinnamon in a small bowl. Spread onto bacon and enjoy this magical moment. Thick cut bacon takes too long for me, so I stick to regular bacon.

Bake for 18-20 min. Do not burn, watch carefully. Cool completely on a parchment-lined plate.

Variations – Mix it up and top the bacon with one of the following: general tsao sauce, taco seasoning, peanut butter, bbq seasoning.

JAY KINNEY

\-

EASY ENTREES

BEEF AND BARLEY STEW

Makes 4-6 servings

DO NOT DOUBLE

1 T. butter

1 T. olive oil

2 lbs. beef chuck roast, 1 ½" cubes

Kosher salt

Fresh ground black pepper

2 small carrots, peeled and chopped

1 celery rib, chopped

1 medium onion, chopped

½ t. dried thyme

½ t. Hungarian paprika

2 c. Shiraz or Chianti red wine

2 bay leaves

4 c. beef stock

1 c. pearl barley

JAY KINNEY

-

Heat oven to 275. Trace and cut a parchment circle for a cast iron
Dutch oven. Heat a burner to med. High. Add butter and oil.
Season and sear beef in batches. Add the next 6 items and season.
Sauté for 8 min. Raise heat and deglaze with wine.

Scrape up the fond. Raise heat to a simmer, add bay leaves, beef
and stock. Cover with the parchment round and oven braise for 2
hours. Toss the paper and adjust the seasoning. Add barley (and
1 c. water if it's too dry). Cover and cook 40- 45 min. longer.

If you use quick cooking barley, only cook 10-15 min longer.

*Cast iron pot and pans will serve you very well in the kitchen.
The Lodge company is my go-to for cast iron. Wash with a mild
soap and rinse. Dry with paper towels.

Apply 2 T. canola oil and a bunch of kosher salt. Use the paper
towels to swish the salt around. Discard and apply 2 T. canola oil
to re-season.

Lay two paper towels under the lid so the cast iron can "breathe."
This prevents it from rusting in storage.

BEEF BARBACOA

Makes 8 10 servings

4 lbs. boneless beef chuck roast

2 T. olive oil

6 cloves garlic, halved lengthwise

2 t. kosher salt

1 medium onion, chopped

2 t. ground cumin

2 t. dried oregano, crushed

2 chipotles, finely chopped

½ bunch cilantro

1 (14.5 oz.) can fire roasted salsa

Juice of 1 lime

½ c. beef stock

2 bay leaves

-

Heat oven to 325. Cut 12 slits in the roast and stuff w/ garlic.
Season with salt and pepper.   Heat the oil in a large Dutch oven.
Stick with an enamel-lined Dutch oven instead of cast iron.   Sear
off the roast 4-6 min per side.

Once you sear off the second side, add the next 7 items.   Add the
tomatoes, cook for 1-2 min. Add the chipotles, vinegar and stock,
bring to a simmer. Cover and braise for 3 – 3 ½ hrs.

Toss the thyme and bay. Shred the beef and add some of the
juices. You can chill this mixture up to 5 days.

Use beef for barbacoa, empanadas, tacos, burritos, quesadillas, the
list could go on and on.

BEEF PASTIES

Makes 1 dozen pasties

1 small rutabaga, finely chopped

1 large carrot, finely chopped

1 medium onion, finely chopped

4 medium potatoes, finely chopped

2 lbs. ground sirloin, browned off, drained

Kosher salt

Black pepper

Dry thyme

Bacon fat

Egg wash

3 ½ c. flour

2 sticks cold unsalted butter, cubed

5 T. ice water

2 large egg yolks

2 T. distilled white vinegar

1 t. iodized salt

Dried thyme

For the dough, mix all 7 ingredients in a food processor.   Chill for 4 hours.   Roll out 12 pieces.

Stuff with filling, crimp, vent and brush with egg wash.

Bake at 375 for 30-40 min. or until they are golden brown.

BISON CHILI

Makes 2 quarts

2 T. extra virgin olive oil

1 medium onion, finely chopped

1 red bell pepper, finely chopped

3 garlic cloves, minced

1 lb. ground bison

1 T. + 1 t. chili powder

1 ½ t. ground cumin

1 ½ t. dried oregano

1 (28 oz.) can crushed tomatoes in puree

1/3 c. tomato paste

1 (15 oz.) mild chili beans, drained

1 ½ c. low sodium beef stock

1 T. adobo sauce from canned chipotles

Heat a medium saucepot on high heat. Add olive oil, onions and peppers. Sauté for 5 min. Turn down heat to medium. Add the garlic and cook 2 min. Pour into a bowl and set aside.

Brown the bison in the same pot. Drain and pour back in. Add the sautéed vegetables.

Stir in the remaining ingredients. Simmer on medium low heat for 25 min. For chili mac, toss with cooked macaroni and cheese.

Bison is naturally very low in fat, 3g fat per 3 oz. It is packed with lean protein and iron to help your body thrive. The tomatoes also pack a huge nutritional punch because they are known to lower your risk of prostate cancer because of its potent amount of lycopene.

BISON QUINOA STUFFED PEPPERS

Makes 6 servings

2 T. extra virgin olive oil

2 carrots, peeled, finely chopped

1 medium onion, finely chopped

2 celery ribs, finely chopped

2 T. minced garlic

2 c. cooked quinoa*

1 (8 oz.) can tomato sauce

3 T. Italian seasoning

2 T. chicken base

2 T. tomato paste

Kosher salt

Fresh ground black pepper

6 red bell peppers, halved vertically and cored

2 lbs. ground bison

Shredded Muenster cheese

Grease a large roasting pan with cooking spray; set aside. Heat a large skillet on medium high heat. Add the olive oil and the mirepoix.* Sauté for 10 min. but do not burn the onions. Turn heat down to medium. Add the garlic and cook for 3 min.

Add the quinoa, tomato sauce, Italian seasoning, chicken base, tomato paste, salt and pepper. Heat through and pour into a large bowl.

Heat the oven to 375. In the same skillet, add the bison. On medium heat, brown up the meat. Be careful not to overcook the meat here. Add the meat to the bowl and mix.

Lay the peppers in the roasting dish. Add 1 cup water to prevent any burning later on. Stuff the peppers with the bison mixture. Cover with parchment paper and then foil. Bake for 1 hr. Uncover and top with cheese. Bake for 3 min. to melt the cheese.

* Mirepoix is a French term for onions, carrots and celery.

* I prefer the standard white quinoa over red, just my personal preference. Be sure to rinse the quinoa in a sieve before cooking to remove the bitter coating known as saponin. Quinoa is one of the major superfoods today. It packs a long list of nutrients and supplying you with all of the essential amino acids.

BULGOGI

Makes 4-6 servings

¾ c. tamari

3 T. brown sugar

3" ginger, peeled, sliced, crushed

6 garlic cloves, crushed

1 lemongrass stalk, crushed

2 T. scallions, thinly sliced

¼ c. rice wine vinegar

1 t. toasted sesame oil

2 ½ - 3 lbs. rib eye steak or beef tenderloin, thinly sliced

Puree the marinade in a blender until its smooth. Chill and marinate the steak for at least 2 hrs. Drain and pat dry. Stir fry on med high heat for 3-5 min. keep in mind small slices of steak cook fast!

Serve on brioche slider buns and Thai Chile slaw. (Mix shredded cabbage, scallions and carrots with Thai Chile Ginger Vinaigrette from Superb Sauces).

CHICKEN CACCIATORE

Makes 4 servings

6 slices bacon, 1/2" pieces

8 skin on bone in chicken thighs, trimmed

1 medium onion, chopped

1 red bell pepper, 2" strips

1 carrot, peeled, thinly sliced

1 celery rib, chopped

3 garlic cloves, minced

4 ½ t. AP flour

1 1/3 c. dry white wine

1 c. chicken stock

1 (14.5 oz.) can diced tomatoes w/ juice

1 T. fresh thyme, finely chopped

1 T. fresh oregano, finely chopped

Cook the bacon on medium heat in a Dutch oven for 7-10 min. Save 1 T. fat. Heat to medium high heat and add the chicken thighs in batches. Cook for 5 min per side. Cool slightly, toss the skin. Drain and save 1 ½ T fat. Add the onions, carrots, peppers and celery. Sauté for 6 min. Add garlic, cook 1 min. Season with salt and pepper.

Deglaze with wine and scrape up the fond. Add the stock, tomatoes and half of the bacon. Mix and then add the chicken.

Cover and bring to a simmer. Simmer for 30 min. Add remaining bacon. Simmer for 5 min. until the chicken is very tender. Add the herbs.

You can omit the bacon and use olive oil to cook the vegetables.

CHIPOTLE LIME CHICKEN

Makes 6 servings

1 c. lime juice

1 T. adobo sauce from canned chipotles

½ t. smoked paprika

1 T. honey

1 t. roasted garlic powder

½ t. cumin

2 T. olive oil

½ t. kosher salt

6 boneless skinless chicken breasts

Puree the first 8 items in a blender. Pour into a bowl and add the chicken. Chill for 2-4 hours. Leave the chicken out at room temp. for 30 min. Heat oven to 375 and line a baking sheet with parchment paper. Drain off and discard the marinade. Roast the chicken off until it is 165. Rest for 10 min. then slice.

Note: You may butterfly the chicken to cook it faster.

CROCKPOT CARNITAS

7-8 lb. pork butt, trimmed and rubbed with taco seasoning and stuffed with garlic in 8 little pockets

2 bay leaves

1 (28 oz.) can enchilada sauce

2 limes, juiced

2 T. brown sugar

1 yellow onion, sliced

1 chipotle in adobo, plus 2 T. sauce

2 c. chicken stock

Spread the bottom of a large crockpot. Add the remaining ingredients in the listed order. Cover and cook on low for 8-9 hrs. Chop and use in empanadas, enchiladas, nachos, burritos.

This does freeze very well.

JAY KINNEY

ENDLESS EMPANADAS

Makes 3 dozen empanadas

2 T. extra virgin olive oil

1 medium onion, grated

½ green bell pepper, minced

½ red bell pepper, minced

3 garlic cloves, minced

2 t. ground cumin

¼ t. cayenne

1 lb. ground bison

Taco seasoning to taste

1 c. beef stock

3 c. all-purpose flour

1 c. masa harina

1 t. granulated sugar

2 t. iodized salt

2 t. ground turmeric

1 ½ sticks unsalted butter, cut into small pieces and chilled

1 c. ice cold water

4 T. canola oil

1 large egg + 1 T. whole milk

Heat the oil in a 12" nonstick skillet on med heat. Cook and stir the onions 5 min. Add in the garlic, cumin, and cayenne cook 1 min. Cook and stir in the bison, brown off for 7-8 min. Add the beef stock and simmer 3-5 min. Pour into a bowl and cool 10 min. Chill for 1 hr.

Blitz 1 c. flour, masa, salt and sugar. Pulse in the butter so it looks like wet sand. Pulse in the remaining flour. Pour into a bowl and sprinkle the liquids on top. Mix until a tacky dough forms. Cut in half and cut each half into 6 pieces. Cover and chill for 45 min.

Heat oven to 375. Line two baking sheets with parchment paper. Roll out each dough piece into a 3" circle. Cover briefly to keep them moist. Spoon filling onto each circle. Brush the edges w/ water and fold over. Crimp the edges w/ a fork. Poke a few holes on top. Brush them w/ olive oil.

Lay the empanadas on each pan. Bake 15-20 min. until they are golden brown.

*Blitz is a term used for running through a food processor.

GARLIC HERB CHICKEN LEGS

Makes 4 servings

2 heads garlic

2 fresh thyme sprigs

2 rosemary sprigs

Onion powder

¼ c. + 2 T extra virgin olive oil

Kosher salt

Black pepper

4 chicken legs, preferably Bell & Evans brand from Nino Salvaggio

Heat oven to 350. Cut off the stem end of the garlic. Pop into a baking dish, add the herbs and drizzle with 2 T. oil. Cover tightly w foil. Roast for 40-45 min. Cool, puree the garlic meat, herbs, ¼ c oil, salt & pepper. Use for chicken, beef, lamb, shrimp, fish or pork.

ITALIAN POT ROAST

Makes 6-8 servings

4 ½ lbs. beef chuck roast

1 medium onion, chopped

4 carrots, peeled, chopped

4 celery ribs, chopped

8 garlic cloves, crushed

1 bunch fresh thyme

Kosher salt

28 oz. can whole Italian tomatoes

¼ t each: ground allspice, cinnamon and cloves

2 bay leaves

1 ½ c. Shiraz red wine

½ c. beef stock

Season the beef and sear off in a cast iron Dutch oven with olive oil on med high heat. Once they are browned, lay them into your 5 qt. crockpot.

Sauté the onions for 6 min. Add the carrots, celery, garlic and thyme. Sauté for 2 min. Add spices and bay leaves.

Raise heat to high and deglaze with the wine. Cook down for 5 min. Add the stock and tomatoes, bring to a boil. Pour over the beef and cook on low for 8-9 hours.

MANGO BRAISED RIBS

Makes 4-6 servings

3 ½ lbs. country style ribs or baby back ribs, cut into two pieces

10 oz. jar Major Grey's mango chutney

½ c. Looza mango nectar

14 oz. can whole peeled tomatoes w/ juice

¼ c. lime juice

2 T. light brown sugar

2 T. Dijon mustard

1 T. cider vinegar

1 T. low sodium tamari soy sauce

2 T. adobo sauce

1 t. kosher salt

Lay the ribs, bone side up against the sides of the crockpot, lining it. Add the remaining items to a med saucepan on high heat. Bring to a boil, boil 15 min. and gently mash with a potato masher and the sauce has reduced to 2 ½ c. Cool and pour over ribs. Cover and cook on low for 8 hrs.

Put the ribs on a cutting board and cover with foil. Leave the sauce in for 5 min. then degrease with paper towels. Pour the sauce in a med saucepan and bring to a boil. Cook for 15 min until it's down to 1 ½ cups. Brush onto the ribs.

JAY KINNEY

RAGIN' CAJUN MAC & CHEESE

Makes 4 servings

3 c. whole milk

½ c. butter

½ c. flour

2 t. kosher salt

1 c. grated fontina cheese

½ lb. cavatappi pasta, cooked just under al dente

½ c. chopped roasted red peppers

2 Andouille sausages, cooked and diced

Heat the milk in a medium saucepan on medium heat for 3-4 min. Meanwhile melt the butter in a large saucepan. Whisk in the flour, cook for about 3 min. until the roux is a light brown color. Off heat, slowly whisk in the hot milk, in 3 additions. Put the sauce back on med hi heat and cook 2-3 min. Add salt.

Add the sauce, cheeses and white wine in a large pot on med heat. Stir for 3 min. Add the pasta and cook 5 min., stir constantly. Add the peppers and sausage.

ROASTED CHERRY BBQ CHICKEN

Makes 6 servings

2 qts. water

2 T. kosher salt

¼ c. brown sugar

2 garlic cloves, crushed

4 sprigs thyme

6 chicken legs (L's)

Cherry BBQ Sauce

Mix the brine and add the chicken. Brine for 2-4 hours.

Heat oven to 350. Pat the chicken dry and sear on medium high heat with an olive oil + butter until they're golden brown. Line a roasting pan with foil and a sheet of parchment. Add the seared chicken and add enough water to coat the bottom. Add fresh thyme and cover the dish with foil.

Bake until the chicken hits 165 on a meat thermometer. Drain the water off. Brush the sauce on and bake for 2-3 minutes to caramelize the sauce.

This chicken is fantastic. It will blow your balls off!

SMOKED TURKEY & WILD RICE SOUP

Makes 8 servings

2 medium onions, minced

4 garlic cloves, minced

1 T. tomato paste

1 T. canola oil

½ t. dried thyme

8 c. low sodium chicken stock

3 carrots, peeled, sliced

2 celery ribs, sliced

2 bay leaves

2 bone in smoked turkey thighs (2 lbs.), skinned

Kosher salt

Fresh ground black pepper

1 c. long grain and wild rice blend, Uncle Ben's

2 T. finely chopped parsley

Microwave the onions, tomato paste, garlic, oil and thyme in a bowl for 5 min, stir halfway through. Dump into a slow cooker. Add the stock, carrots, celery and bay leaves. Season the turkey and add in. Cover and cook for 6-8 hrs. on low or 5-7 hrs. on high.

Chop turkey meat and set aside. Leave the soup for 10 min, skim off the fat. Toss the bay leaves. Add in rice, cover and cook on high for 30-40 min. Add turkey, parsley, salt and pepper.

Make a big batch and freeze it for those cold winter days. I grew up with Chicken Noodle Soup but this one kicks ass!

SOUTHWEST CHICKEN

Makes 6 servings

1 T. chili powder

2 t. kosher salt

2 t. dried oregano

2 t. dried thyme

2 t. roasted garlic powder

2 t. onion powder

2 t. smoked paprika

1 t. black pepper

¼ c. olive oil

(1 t. cayenne pepper, optional)

6 boneless skinless chicken breasts, trimmed

Mix up the marinade and add the chicken. Cover and chill overnight. Roast at 375 on a parchment lined baking sheet until the chicken is at 165. Rest for at least 10 min. before slicing.

Serve with Mr. Smokey's Salsa.

SUNDAY POT ROAST

Makes 6-8 servings

3 ½ lbs. boneless beef chuck eye roast

Kosher salt

Fresh ground black pepper

2 T. canola oil

1 medium onion, chopped

1 carrot, peeled, chopped

1 celery rib, chopped

2 garlic cloves, minced

2 t. granulated sugar

2 c. dry red wine, Shiraz or Cabernet Sauvignon

1 c. beef stock

1 bunch fresh thyme

Position an oven rack to the middle and heat to 300. Dry off the roast and season. Heat oil in a large Dutch oven on med high. Brown the roast on all sides, 8-10 min. Set aside. Reduce heat to med, add the mirepoix. Cook and stir 6-8 min. Add sugar and garlic, cook 1 min.

Raise heat to high. Deglaze with the wine, reduce down by half. Add the stock and thyme, scrape up the fond. Add the roast and water to come halfway up the sides of the roast. Cover the pot with foil then cover with lid.

Bring to a simmer and throw into the oven for 3 ½ - 4 hrs. Rest the beef under foil for 10 min. Toss the thyme and skim off the fat. Boil the liquid down to 1 ½ cups, about 8 min. Add the wine and reduce for 2-3 min. Season and serve with the beef. Roast vegetables separately (potatoes, carrots, etc.)

TROPICAL CHICKEN STIR FRY

Makes 2 servings

2" ginger, crushed

2 garlic clove, crushed

1 t. sesame oil

1 c. Kikkoman Stir Fry Sauce

2 T. honey

2 T. Thai Chile sauce

1 large chicken breast

½ c. fresh pineapple, small diced

½ red bell pepper, julienned

¼ c. carrots, julienned

¼ c. baby corn

1 scallion, white part thinly sliced

3 shiitake mushrooms, stemmed and sliced

Whisk the first 6 ingredients in a small bowl. Pour ½ in another bowl, wrap and chill. Slice the chicken into strips across the grain. This will ensure a consistently juicy piece of chicken.

Add to the marinade and mix. Cover with plastic wrap and chill for 2 hrs. Drain off the marinade and pat the chicken dry.

Heat a large skillet on high heat. Add a small amount of canola oil. Stir fry the chicken, in two batches, until it's cooked through. Pour into a bowl and set aside.

Wipe out the skillet and put it back on high heat. Add canola oil and pineapple. Stir fry for 2 min. Add the remaining vegetables. Stir fry until the vegetables are crisp-tender.

Turn the heat down to medium. Pour in the reserved marinade. Cook for 1 min.

For each serving, spoon the rice into bowls. Pour the chicken and vegetables on top. Serve with Aromatic Rice.

SIDEKICKS

AROMATIC RICE

Makes 4 servings

1 ½ c. brown rice, short or medium grain

1 lemongrass stalk, split and crushed

3" ginger, sliced

2 ½ cups water

2 T. olive oil

1 t. kosher salt

Heat oven to 375. Dump the rice, lemongrass and ginger in an 8" glass baking dish. Bring the water to a boil on high heat. Add the oil and salt. Pour the hot water over the rice.

Cover tightly with heavy duty foil. Bake for 1 hr.

BISON GYOZA

Makes 50 dumplings

1 lb. ground bison

50 wonton wrappers

2 T. Thai Chile Sauce

2 T. minced garlic

2 T. minced ginger

(1/4 t cinnamon)

¼ c minced carrots

½ c minced onions

2-3 egg yolks

1 T. sesame oil

Cook the onions and carrots in sesame oil.   Add the ginger, garlic and lemongrass, cook 2 min. Cool. Mix with bison and eggs. Add the Thai Chile Sauce.

Stuff and deep fry in peanut oil. Serve with Tangy Tangerine Sauce.

BROCCOLI BOURSIN RISOTTO

FRITTERS

Makes 4-6 servings

5-5 ½ c. low sodium chicken stock

2 T. olive oil

1/3 c. shallots, minced

1 ½ c. Arborio rice (short grain Italian rice)

1 lb. broccoli, cut into small florets

1 (5.2 oz.) pkg. Boursin cheese

1/3 c. mascarpone cheese

2 T. minced chives

Heat stock just below a simmer on medium heat. In a medium saucepot, heat the olive oil to medium high heat. Sauté the shallots until they are translucent, 2-3 min. Add the rice and toast for 2 min.

Stir in ½ c. stock. Continue to stir in ½ c. additions of stock. The rice should be al dente, but not crunchy, after 25 min. Stir in the broccoli, cheeses, and chives off heat. Pour the risotto into a greased jelly roll pan (the large surface area helps hot food cool down quickly, this works well for cooling down quinoa too).

For the Risotto Fritters:

1 c. all-purpose flour

3 large eggs, beaten

2 c. Panko bread crumbs

Olive oil

Shape the risotto into ¾" cakes. Lay them on a parchment lined baking sheet. Set up three shallow dishes with flour, eggs and panko, in that order.

Heat a large skillet on medium high heat. Add 2 T. olive oil and add the cakes. Brown off the cakes in batches. Each batch should take 5 min. turning once. This makes a great vegetarian entrée or even a great side dish to roast chicken.

Risotto cakes would have to be the closest thing to vegetarian dinner that I can think of. I'm not a fan of tofu or soy products in general, I guess I can see those soybeans getting ground into juice! Remember, not all meat is bad.

Stick to grass fed and free range meats. Buy meats from reputable stores such as Butcher Boy, Nino Salvaggio, Randazzos.

You can shop at Whole Foods but keep in mind that if you buy everything organic, your shopping trips will be known as "Whole Paycheck." With nutrition, the more you know, the more you don't want to know. Don't let the foods stress you out. Eat a wide balanced diet and be happy.

If not, you may become a walking shadow.

JAY KINNEY

GARLIC CHEESE BISCUITS

Makes 1 dozen

2 c. AP flour

4 t. baking powder

½ t. baking soda

½ t. granulated sugar

¾ t. iodized salt

2 T. roasted garlic powder

2 T. Italian seasoning

1 c. grated extra sharp cheddar cheese

½ c. unsalted butter, chopped, chilled

¾ - 1 c. buttermilk, chilled

Heat oven to 375. Line a baking sheet with parchment paper. Arrange an oven rack to the top shelf.

Mix the dry ingredients and cheddar cheese together in a large bowl (you may also do this in a food processor). Cut in the butter until they are pea-sized. Make a well and pour in ¾ c. buttermilk (you may need more if it's a cloudy day). Stir just until it forms a dough. Knead briefly on a lightly floured surface.

Roll out to ½" thick and cut into biscuits, round or square. Brush with whole milk and bake for 13-15 minutes or until they are golden brown. Cool completely on a wire rack.

118

GARLIC HERB YUKON WEDGES

Makes 6 servings

10- 12 medium Yukon Gold potatoes, washed and quartered

Roasted garlic powder

Onion powder

Kosher salt

Fresh ground black pepper

Dried thyme

Dried oregano

Extra virgin olive oil

Heat oven to 375. Roast the potatoes on a parchment lined baking sheet until they are golden brown and tender.

KALE WITH GARLIC & GINGER

Makes 4 servings

2 T. olive oil

2 garlic cloves, sliced

2" ginger, sliced

Pinch of red chili flakes

½ bunch kale, stemmed, chopped (4-5 cups)

1 c. chicken stock

Heat a large deep skillet on medium heat. Add the oil and swirl to coat the pan. Cook the garlic, ginger and chili flakes for 2 min.

Add the kale and stock. Cover and bring to a boil. Cook for 5 min. Uncover and let the stock evaporate. The kale should be tender and deep green.

This is way tastier than drinking kale!

PINEAPPLE MANGO CHUTNEY

Makes 3 cups

1 c. mango nectar

1 ½ t. minced fresh ginger

8 baby stalks lemongrass, bottom 1" pieces crushed and wrapped in cheesecloth

1 (12 oz.) bag frozen mango, thawed

1 (16 oz.) bag frozen pineapple, thawed

2 T. orange blossom honey

Boil everything on med high heat for 15 min. Toss the lemongrass and puree.

JAY KINNEY

QUICK QUINOA

Makes 6-8 servings

2 c. quinoa, rinsed and drained

2 c. water

2 T. chicken base

3 sprigs fresh thyme

2 garlic cloves, crushed

Dump all five ingredients in a medium saucepot. Cover and turn heat to high. Once it comes to a boil, drop heat to medium. Simmer for 15 min. Set the pot aside 5 minutes to steam. This will keep for up to 5 days.

*Feel free to omit the garlic and thyme, add ginger and lemongrass instead. Use your imagination to spruce up dinner.

SAFFRON RICE

Makes 4-6 servings

2 T. olive oil

1 yellow onion, diced

1 green pepper, diced

1 red pepper, diced

1 ½ c. Arborio rice

2-3 c. chicken stock

½ t. saffron threads, crushed

Bloom the saffron in 1 T. hot water; set aside. Sauté the onions in oil in a large skillet on medium high heat.   Add the peppers and cook 5 min. Add the rice, stock and saffron. Cook 15-20 min. uncovered. Season and cool.

JAY KINNEY

BONUS RECIPES

ANDOUILLE SAUSAGE

Makes l lb.

1 lb. ground pork

2-3 T. cup That Red Stuff seasoning

1 t. minced garlic

1/2 t. fresh ground pepper

1/2 t. kosher salt

Mix the pork with the remaining ingredients. Chill overnight.

CHORIZO SAUSAGE

Makes 1 lb.

1 lb. ground pork

3 oz. bacon fat

1 chipotle in adobo sauce, finely chopped

2 t. granulated garlic

1 t. ground cumin

1 T. kosher salt

2 t. granulated onion

1 t. Hungarian or Spanish paprika

1 t. dried oregano

Mix and chill overnight.   You may also shape and freeze for up to 3 months.

CINNAMON ROLLS

Makes 12 rolls

½ c. whole milk

1 stick unsalted butter

½ c. warm water (110-115 degrees)

2 ½ t. active dry yeast

¼ c. granulated sugar

1 large egg + 2 egg yolks

1 ½ t. iodized salt

4-4 ¼ c. all-purpose flour

8 oz. cream cheese, softened

2 T. honey

2 T. heavy cream

1 c. powdered sugar, sifted

1 t. vanilla extract

Pinch of iodized salt

¾ c. light brown sugar

3 T. cinnamon

Pinch of iodized salt

Heat the milk and butter in a saucepan. Set aside and cool until its 100 degrees. Mix the water, yeast, sugar, eggs and yolks on low speed. Add the salt, warm milk and 2 c flour on med speed. Switch to the dough hook and add another 2 c flour. Knead until the dough is smooth and elastic, 10 min. Proof in a lightly greased bowl for 1 ½-2 hrs.

For the icing, mix everything on low speed. Raise up to high speed for 2 min. Chill for later.

Roll out the dough to a 16x12" rectangle, long side facing you. Mix up the filling and spread out leaving a ½" border. Roll up and seal the edges w/ water. Grease a 13X9" pan and cut the rolls. Lay them in the pan and cover w/ plastic. Proof for 1 ½ - 2 hrs. Heat oven to 350 and position an oven rack to the middle.

Bake for 25-30 min. Cool completely and apply the icing.

GRANOLA

Makes 6 servings

1 ½ c. old-fashioned oats

¼ c. raw honey

1 t. ground cinnamon

½ c. sliced almonds

¼ c. unsweetened coconut flakes

¼ c. sunflower seeds

¼ c. chia seeds

¼ c. wheat germ

½ c. dried cherries

Heat oven to 300.   Line a large baking sheet with parchment paper.

Mix the first 8 ingredients in a large bowl using vinyl gloves (sticky business). Pour the oat mixture onto the prepared pan and spread out evenly.

Bake for 25 min., stir halfway through. Cool completely and mix in the cherries. This will keep for 1 week at room temp.

HONEY WHEAT BREAD

Makes 2 loaves

4 c. bread flour

1 c. whole wheat flour

2 ½ t. active dry yeast

2 c. whole milk*, scalded, (105-115)

1/3 c. canola oil

½ c. honey

2 t. iodized salt*

Milk

Mix the flours and yeast in a mixing bowl. Add the salt, honey, oil and milk. Mix on low speed for 2 min to form a dough. Increase to medium speed and knead for 5 min. until it's smooth and elastic.

Throw in a greased bowl, cover and proof for 1 hr. Punch and cut in half. Roll into a ball, cover and rest 20 min. Grease two 9" loaf pans. Work the dough into an 8 X 12" rectangle. Rollup, pop in pan and brush with milk.

Proof uncovered for 1 hr. Heat oven to 400. Bake 40-50 min. Pop out at once and cool.

*Rinse out a small saucepan with cold water before you add the milk. This will prevent the milk from scorching.

HOT COCOA MIX

Makes 3 ½ cups

1 T. ground cinnamon

½ c. Dutch-processed cocoa powder

1 c. non-dairy coffee creamer

2 c. powdered sugar

Stir 1/3 c. mix + 3/4 c. hot water or whole milk. Let it cool for at least 5 min. Don't burn your tongue.

HUMMUS

Makes 2 cups

16 oz. can chickpeas, drained

1/3 c. fresh Meyer lemon juice

¼ c tahini (sesame seed paste)

2 garlic cloves, minced

1/2 t. ground cumin

Kosher salt

Blitz all seven ingredients in a food processor. Feel free to get creative here. Add more cumin, tahini, garlic, etc. Chill for 2 hours to mellow out the flavors. This will keep for 3 days. Before serving, top with a little extra virgin olive oil. This little tip will improve your health, ask the Greeks!

INDIAN SPICE MIX

Makes 2 ½ Tablespoons

1 T. Hungarian paprika

½ t. smoked paprika

1 t. kosher salt

½ t. ground ginger

½ t. ground cumin

½ t. ground coriander

½ t. ground turmeric

¼ t. granulated garlic

Mix and rub on salmon, chicken, pork or shrimp.

ITALIAN SAUSAGE

Makes 1 lb.

1 lb. ground pork

1 t. minced garlic

1 T. Hungarian paprika

2 t. kosher salt

½ t. roasted garlic powder

¼ t. onion powder

¼ t. black pepper

1 T. Italian seasoning

2 T. dry red wine

Mix in a large bowl and chill overnight. Cook to 155. Freeze raw or cooked up to 3 months.

I like to make my own sausage so that I can control the sodium and seasonings going in. I really don't care for fennel seed, so I leave it out here.

ROSEMARY KALAMATA OLIVE BREAD

Makes 2 loaves

2 1/2 c. AP flour

1 T. fast rising yeast

1 t. each: dried rosemary, thyme, oregano

1/2 T. roasted garlic powder

1 t. fresh ground black pepper

1 c. water

1/4 c. extra virgin olive oil

3-4 T. honey

1/2-1 cup Kalamata olives, chopped, rinsed, drained and patted dry

3 T. olive oil or garlic herb oil

Mix the dry ingredients and olives in a mixing bowl. Heat the three liquids to 120-125 degrees.

Add the warm liquid mixture in and combine with a dough hook. Once a dough forms, knead for 8-10 minutes until it becomes smooth and elastic. Cover and proof in a warm place for 30 minutes.

Punch down and shape into loaves or rolls. (For a fancier presentation, score the dough to help it rise.) Cover with a damp towel and proof for another 30 minutes.

Bake at 400 degrees for 30-35 minutes or until it sounds hollow. It should also reach 190-205 degrees inside. After 15 min., brush oil on to create a golden brown crust.

Cool completely before slicing. You can also use this dough for pizza and calzones.

MANGO COCONUT OATMEAL

Makes 1 serving

½ c. rolled oats

1 c. water

2 T. raw honey

¼ t. ground cinnamon

1/3 c. frozen mangoes, thawed

2 T. sweetened coconut flakes, toasted

Mix the oats and water in a small saucepan. Bring to a boil on medium heat and cook for 5 min. Add the honey, cinnamon and mangoes. Cook for 2 min.

Sprinkle the toasted coconut on top.

PUMPKIN PIE SCONES

Makes 10 scones

2 c. whole wheat flour

1 T. baking powder

2 t. ground cinnamon

½ t. ground nutmeg

Dash of ground cloves & ginger

½ t iodized salt

1/3 c. cold unsalted butter

1/3 c. light brown sugar

1 c. canned pumpkin puree

1/3 c. whole milk

1 t. vanilla extract

Whisk the dry items. Cut in the butter. Chill for 15 min. Whisk the wet items. Add to the flour mix. Knead briefly until the dough comes together.

Shape into a 9" circle ¾" thick. Cut into 10 wedges and lay on a parchment lined baking sheet.

Bake at 400 for 13-17 min. or until a toothpick comes out clean.

THAT RED STUFF

Makes 1 ½ cups

1/3 c. kosher salt

1/3 c. chili powder

1/3 c. Old Bay seasoning

2 T. onion powder

2 T. smoked paprika

1 T. garlic powder

1 T. dried oregano

2 T. ground cumin

Mix and use to season meats such as beef, chicken or pork.

I made this during my early days in high school. I would sit down to eat lunch and open up a bag of That Red Stuff. My peers asked if I would share.

Before I knew it, the entire lunch room was passing this bag of seasoning around. Eventually I emptied out garlic powder containers for sheer convenience. "Let me have some of That Red Stuff!"

TURKEY PEPPERONI & CHEESE ROLLS

Makes 1 dozen

1 c. whole milk

1/2 c. water

1/4 c. unsalted butter

3 1/2 cups AP flour

3 T. granulated sugar

1 t. iodized salt

4 1/2 t. fast rising yeast

Olive oil

Italian seasoning

Roasted garlic powder

Shredded mozzarella cheese

Sliced pepperoni, turkey or regular

Mix the flour, sugar, salt and yeast in a large mixing bowl with a dough hook attachment. Pour the milk, water and butter in a glass Pyrex cup.

Microwave on High for 1 1/2 minutes or until its 120-125 degrees. Gradually mix into the flour mixture on low speed. Mix for 1 minute.

Add more flour, gradually, 1/2 cup at a time. However, you don't want to add more than 1 1/2 cups otherwise your dough will be too dry.

Humidity will play a big part when making breads and doughs. Baking bread on a warm, sunny day is your best bet.

Knead 8 minutes by hand or with the mixer until its smooth and elastic. Turnover in a greased bowl. Cover with a moist towel and proof 30-60 minutes in a warm spot. The dough should double in size.

Punch down and cut into 12 pieces. Roll each piece out to 7" in diameter. Fill with pepperoni and cheese. Roll and seal up the edges. Cover and proof 30 minutes, until they have increased in size again.

Brush each roll with olive oil. Top with Italian seasoning and garlic.

Bake at 375 for 10-12 minutes. They should be lightly browned and a toothpick should come out clean.

ULTIMATE OATMEAL

Makes 1 serving

½ c. rolled oats (steel cut oats are for horses)

1 c. water

2 T. raw honey

¼ t. ground cinnamon

1 t. chia seeds

Mix the oats and water in a small saucepan. Bring to a boil and cook for 5 min. Add the honey and cinnamon. Cook for 2 min. Cool for 5 min. then add your chia seeds. I like my oatmeal thick and rough.

For a boost, add dried cherries, peanut butter, almond butter, chocolate or dried blueberries.

Don't take vitamins, just eat chia seeds.

142

WILD BLUEBERRY MUFFINS

Makes 1 dozen

3 c. + 2 T. cake flour

2 t. baking powder

1 t. baking soda

Heavy pinch iodized salt

1 c. granulated sugar

1/2 c. canola oil

1 large egg

1 c. vanilla yogurt

1 1/2 c. frozen wild blueberries, thawed and drained or fresh blueberries

Zest of 1 Meyer lemon

Cinnamon sugar

Preheat oven to 400.

In a large bowl sift together the flour, baking soda, baking powder, and salt. Set aside.

In another large bowl, whisk together the sugar, oil, egg, lemon zest and yogurt. Add the dry ingredients reserving 1 tablespoon of the dry ingredients and toss with the blueberries.

Stir mixture for only one minute, do not overmix otherwise your muffins will have large tunnels. Add blueberries to mixture and stir 3 more times. Sprinkle cinnamon sugar on top.

Using a #20 ice cream scoop, portion out the batter into greased muffin pans. Sprinkle the remaining 1/2 cup of berries on top of muffins and press down lightly. Bake for 20 to 25 minutes, rotating pan halfway through.

Remove from oven and turn out, upside down on a tea towel to cool completely.

Serve immediately or store in airtight container for 2 to 3 days.

JUST DESSERTS

ALMOND BUTTER NO BAKE COOKIES

Makes 2 dozen

1 stick unsalted butter

½ c. almond butter

1 ¾ c. vanilla granulated sugar

½ c. whole milk

¼ c. Dutch processed cocoa powder

2 t. vanilla extract

3 c. rolled oats

Melt the butters in a medium saucepan on medium high heat. Stir in the sugar until it dissolves. Add the milk, cocoa, vanilla and oats. Bring to a full boil and cook for 90 seconds. Quickly drop the no bake mixture onto a greased sheet of parchment paper using greased table spoons.

Store for up to 1 week in an airtight container between layers of parchment paper.

APPLE CINNAMON BREAD PUDDING

Makes 9 servings

2 c. heavy cream

2 c. whole milk

1 c. granulated sugar

9 large egg yolks

¾ t. iodized salt

Ground cinnamon

Ground nutmeg

2 large Granny Smith apples, peeled, cored and chopped

1 loaf challah bread, stale, cubed (9 cups)

Heat oven to 350. Grease a 13 x 9" pan with cooking spray. In a large bowl, whisk together the first 7 ingredients. Add the apples and bread.

Bake the pudding for 45-50 min. Serve with Rum Caramel.

APPLE PIE BARS

Makes 12 servings

2 c. quick oats

½-3/4 c. brown sugar

¼ t. iodized salt

1 t. ground cinnamon

¼ t. ground nutmeg

¼ t. ground ginger

2 c. dried apples, chopped

¼ c. shredded sweetened coconut

¼ c. toasted pecans

1 t. vanilla extract

¼ c. + 2 T. melted butter

½ c. + 2 T. honey

1 T. water

Heat oven to 350.

Line a large baking sheet with parchment paper. Mix the dry ingredients, apples, coconut and pecans. Mix the wet ingredients and add to the dry mixture. Adjust the sugar to your taste.

Bake for 22-25 min or until its golden brown. Cool completely and cut into bars. Chill for up to 1 week.

BELGIAN CHOCOLATE CHUNK COOKIES

Makes 2 dozen

2 sticks unsalted butter, softened

1 ¾ c. light brown sugar

2 t. vanilla extract

2 large eggs, beaten

2 ½ c. all-purpose flour

¾ t. iodized salt

1 ½ t. baking soda

1 ¼ c. dark Belgian chocolate, finely chopped

Heat oven to 375. Cream the butter and sugar in a large bowl. Stir in the vanilla and eggs. Mix the flour, salt and soda in a small bowl. Gradually mix in the flour mixture in three additions. Stir in the chocolate.

Line 3 cookie sheets with parchment. Roll out walnut-sized balls of dough and lay them 2" apart. Bake 10-12 minutes. Cool for 3 minutes then transfer to a wire rack to cool completely. Munch on these for up to 1 week or freeze for up to 1 year.

DARK CHOCOLATE ICE CREAM

Makes 2 quarts

1 c. Dutch processed cocoa, preferably Rodelle

2/3 c. granulated sugar

½ c. brown sugar

1 ½ c. whole milk

3 ¼ c. heavy cream

1 vanilla bean, scraped

Whisk the cocoa and sugars. Whisk in the liquids and chill at least 12 hours and freeze an ice cream maker bowl and paddle. Turn the ice cream machine on BEFORE you add the mix. Let it run for 2 min.

Slowly pour in the cream mixture. Churn for 15-20 min.

FUDGE BROWNIES

Makes 9 brownies

1 ½ sticks unsalted butter

4 oz. unsweetened chocolate, chopped

2 large eggs, beaten

1 1/3 c. granulated sugar

2 t. vanilla extract

¼ t. iodized salt

¼ c. cake flour, sifted

Toasted NUTS, chopped

Heat oven to 350 and grease a 9" square baking pan. Line it with parchment paper. Melt the butter and chocolate in the microwave in 15-20 sec intervals, stir occasionally.

Whip the eggs, vanilla, sugar and salt for 4-5 min on high speed until its thick and light. While stirring, pour some egg mix into the chocolate to lighten it up. Then pour the chocolate into the egg mix on med speed. Mix in the flour and nuts. Pour and spread out into the pan. Bake for 30-40 min.

KAHLUA CRÈME BRULEE

Makes 6 servings

6 large eggs, separated

1 c. granulated sugar

2 c. heavy cream, preferably 40% fat content

1/3 c. Kahlua

1/3 c. Bailey's

1 vanilla bean, split and scraped

1/8 t. kosher salt

Whisk the egg yolks, sugar, salt and vanilla together into a thick paste. Whisk in the heavy cream. Strain and pour into 6 or more ramekins in a large roasting pan. Pour 1-1 ½" very hot water into the large roasting pan and cover.

Bake at 300 for 60-75 minutes until the custards have set. Chill well.

To serve, sprinkle some granulated sugar on top and brulee.

For a plain vanilla crème brulee, omit the Kahlua and Baileys.

LEMONGRASS LEISURE ICE CREAM

Makes 2 quarts

6 large egg yolks

1 ½ c. heavy cream, divided

1 ½ c. whole milk

¾ c. granulated sugar

Kosher salt

2 vanilla beans, split and scraped

4 lemongrass stalks, crushed

Whisk the yolks in a bowl. Pour 1 c. cream in another bowl, set a strainer on top. Whisk the milk, sugar, salt and ½ c. cream in a medium saucepan.

Bring to a simmer. Slowly whisk this mix into the egg yolks. Return the tempered mix back to the saucepan and constantly stir on medium low heat until its 160-170, don't boil (approx. 5 min.). Pour into the strainer and cool. Chill overnight.

Freeze ice cream bowl and paddle overnight. Turn the machine on and let it run for 2 min. Slowly pour in the cream mixture. Churn and freeze for 15-20 min.

For vanilla ice cream, omit the lemongrass.

NO BAKE MONKEY BARS

Makes 15 bars

1 ½ c. peanut butter, preferably Smart Balance

1 ½ c. raw honey

2 T. vanilla extract

1/2 t. ground cinnamon

1 c. dark chocolate chips

1 c. sliced almonds, toasted

1 c. sweetened coconut flakes, toasted

1/4 c. Dutch-processed cocoa powder

6 c. crisp rice cereal

(¼ c. chia seeds)

This recipe is best done using a Kitchen Aid mixer, save your arms!

Cream the peanut butter and honey. Stir in the next 6 ingredients. Slowly add in the cereal in 4 additions.

Spread onto a greased large baking sheet. Press down firmly with greased parchment paper. Sprinkle the chia seeds on top. Chill 30 min. then cut into bars. Keep chilled for up to 1 week or freeze for longer storage.

PUMPKIN SPICE BREAD PUDDING

Makes 6 servings

1 c. heavy cream

1 c. whole milk

2 c. canned pure pumpkin

1 c. brown sugar

2 large eggs + 1 egg yolk

1 ½ t. ground cinnamon

1 ½ t. pumpkin pie spice

2 t. pure vanilla extract

1 loaf challah bread, stale, 1/2" cubes

Whisk the first eight ingredients in a large bowl. Mix in the bread and leave for 20 min. Heat oven to 350. Spray an 8" glass baking dish.

Pour the bread mixture into the greased dish. Bake for 40 min.

Pumpkin Pie Spice Mix

1 ½ t. ground cinnamon

½ t. ground ginger

½ t. ground nutmeg

¼ t. ground cloves

Dash of ground allspice

JAY KINNEY

RUM CUPCAKES

Makes 1 dozen

1 (18.25 oz.) box yellow cake mix

1 (3.4 oz.) box vanilla pudding mix

4 large eggs

½ c. water

½ c. canola oil

½ c. dark rum, preferably Myer's Rum

1 t. ground cinnamon

½ c. unsalted butter

¼ c. water

1 c. vanilla sugar*

½ c. dark rum

Heat oven to 325. Line a standard muffin pan with papers. Add the batter and tap on the counter to remove any air bubbles. Bake for 18-20 min. Cool 5 min. then invert.

Boil the butter, water and sugar for 5 min. Add the rum and brush over the cupcakes. Let the rum glaze soak in overnight. These will keep for 1 month at room temp. in an airtight container or chilled for up to 1 year.

Just don't drink and drive!

*Vanilla sugar is very simple. Take a plastic bag and fill with granulated sugar. Add a vanilla bean and leave for 1 week. Open and enjoy.

For chocolate, use devil's food cake instead of yellow cake mix.

At the time of publication, this costs just under $10 to make. (The famous Tortuga rum cakes run from $15-$40 depending on size.) This will be a hit at your New Year's party. I remember eating a whole batch, and feeling rather buzzed up right after!

SPICY MOLASSES COOKIES

Makes 3 dozen

1 ½ sticks unsalted butter, softened

1 c. packed light brown sugar

1 large egg, beaten

1 t. vanilla extract

⅓ c. unsulfured molasses, preferably Grandma's

2 c. all-purpose flour

1 t. baking soda

½ t. iodized salt

1 t. ground ginger

1 t. ground cloves

2 ¼ t. ground cinnamon

Cream the butter and sugar in a large bowl. Stir in the egg, vanilla and molasses. Mix the flour, soda, salt and spices in a small bowl.

Gradually mix in the flour mixture in 3 additions. Pour into a greased bowl. Cover and chill for 2 hours.

Heat oven to 350. Line three or four cookie sheets with parchment paper. Roll out walnut-size balls of dough and lay them 2" apart. Bake for 11-13 minutes. Munch on these for up to 1 week or freeze for up to 1 year.

FUN FACTS

Honey

- boosts your immunity along with aiding your digestion

-it is effective in helping the body burn fat and curb obesity

- has 22 amino acids

-reduces muscle fatigue

-enhances athletic performance

-aids those with allergies, arthritis and even hangovers

-mix with cinnamon to pump up your immune system

Cinnamon

-helps control blood sugar along with increasing blood circulation

- strong anti-bacterial properties

- relieves gas and bloating

- acts as a food preservative because it inhibits bacterial growth

- has been shown to enhance your memory and cognitive skills
Studies prove that it can fight Alzheimer's

161

-contains antioxidants that fight off free radicals in the body, ironically, stress and oxygen are two huge problems today

- may help lower cholesterol

-can also spice up your love life, wink, wink

Bison

-eating it regularly will reduce your risk for having a stroke and a heart attack

-is jam packed with protein, 28g/ 3.5 oz. serving

- has less fat than chicken, pork and beef, 3g fat/3.5 oz. serving

-has more vitamin b12 than most conventional meats, 2.8 mcg/3.5 oz. serving

- has lots of iron to promote red blood cells

-contains high amounts of selenium, beta carotene and vitamin E

Ginger

-takes down the flu, colds, nausea, infections, indigestion

-reduces muscles fatigue for those active gym rats

-helpful for those with osteoarthritis

-keeps your blood sugar in check as well as your brain and

-very powerful for reducing your risk for heart disease and Alzheimer's

-effective for emptying your stomach quicker

-helps lower your cholesterol

Quinoa

-supplies all nine essential amino acids to make a complete protein, a great choice for vegans and vegetarians

-keeps your mind razor sharp

-high in B vitamins, potassium, magnesium, fiber, protein and zinc

-naturally gluten-free

- a super food loved by the Incas until the Spanish deemed it a major threat to Christianity so they burned the fields

Chia Seeds

-one of the world's superfoods, the Aztecs viewed as more valuable than gold for years until the Spanish conquistadors burned their crops

-great for maintaining as well as losing weight

-supplies close to 1/3 of your daily requirements for dietary fiber

-has the highest amount of plant based omega 3 fatty acid out there

-rich in B vitamins, lots of calcium and potassium

-naturally gluten-free

CHEF TIPS

You are free to add or remove ingredients. Officially, you now have permission. Cooking really is wonderful, experiment with new flavors. To date, I have never followed a recipe all the way through. I am famous for tearing up recipes and perfecting them.

Next time you eat an orange try this. Slice off the peel so you just eat the meat and not the bitter white pith. Take a piece and eat it stem side up first and then the bottom end. The top portion of oranges (or fruits in general) tend to taste sweeter.

Why? When the sun hits the plants, the highest amounts of sugar accumulate in the top thus resulting in a sweeter taste.

For a prank, cut up some blood oranges in February and eat the oranges. Leave the "blood" behind and scare your roommates!

Let's say you are cutting up apples and you realize that you are out of lemons. Soak them in salt water to reduce oxidation. Do you wash it after? Yes!

Have leftover lemons? Throw them in a bowl of water and nuke for 10 minutes on High power. The lemon vapor will strip off any residue inside your microwave.

Add orange peel to raw honey for a cheaper and tastier orange honey.

Out of brown sugar? Combine 1 cup granulated sugar with unsulfured molasses in a mixing bowl. The amount of molasses will depend on your taste. Use less for light, more for regular and even more for dark brown sugar. Use your homemade brown sugar right away.

Does your recipe call for tamarind? Make mock tamarind. Mix equal parts of lime juice and brown sugar in a bowl.   It will have a similar sweet and sour flavor at a much lower price.

Bakers need to use good quality ingredients for consistent results. It is wise to check your baking powder before you start your recipe. Mix a small amount with warm water.

If it bubbles up rapidly, you're good to go. If not, toss it.   I have found that baking powder has a lengthy expiration date. However, I would advise consumers to use it within six months. This tip will also work for yeast too.

ABOUT THE AUTHOR

Chef Jay Kinney has been working in the food service industry since 2006. After graduating from culinary school, he held numerous chef jobs over the years, including the U.S. Army Reserves and the FOOD NETWORK!

He has also been recognized for his cooking tips in Cuisine Magazine. In his spare time, he enjoys cooking, writing and eating enormous amounts of bacon. Jay currently resides in Michigan.

chefjaykinney@yahoo.com

Even more free recipes!

baconmanrecipes.blogspot.com

57055145R00092

Made in the USA
Charleston, SC
06 June 2016